TALKABOUT: SCHOOL

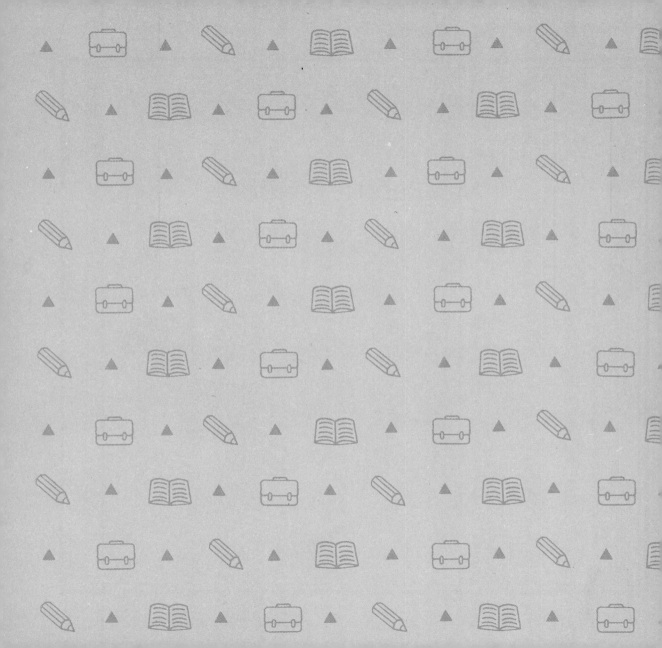

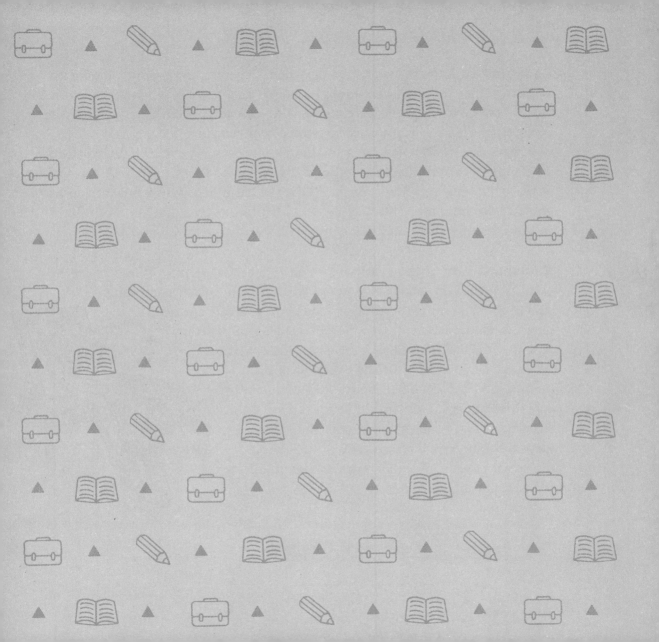

Ladybird Talkabout Books are designed for young children to share with someone older. A child who doesn't read yet can enjoy looking at the books alone, but the greatest pleasure and benefit will come from talking about the pictures. Each book is intended to prompt conversation, to encourage observation and awareness, and to stimulate vocabulary and the imagination. The simple text will lead naturally to discussion of the pictures. As you look at the book together, don't hurry. Allow the child to associate freely, and let yourself do the same. You may be delighted to discover that you both find new things to explore and talk about with every fresh reading.

Talkabout School shows what goes on in a school setting. Whether the child is already in school or is about to start, you'll find many things to talk about here. If the child is in school, you can discuss how the school in the book is like his or hers or different from it. If the child will soon be going to school, the book can help prepare for the experience. Each picture is full of details to notice and comment on, and there are many opportunities to reinforce basic skills like counting and color and shape identification. You'll also be able to talk about the social aspects of school, such as listening, sharing, and helping.

The author thanks the following schools, all in New York City:
the Goddard-Riverside Community Center, the West Side YMCA, and the Dalton Schools.

LADYBIRD BOOKS, INC. Auburn, Maine 04210 U.S.A.
© LADYBIRD BOOKS LTD 1988 Loughborough, Leicestershire, England

School

by ELLEN RUDIN
illustrated by KELLY OECHSLI

Ladybird Books

"Good morning," says the teacher.

TODAY IS TUESDAY

4

Talk about the picture.

Do you see another teacher in the room?

These are the children in the class.
Can you count how many there are?

1

Jennifer

2

Allison

3

Mary

4

Kai

5

Daniel

6

Kate

7

Lori

8

Alden

9

Bess

10

Anna

11

Zachary

12

Ben

In free time the children can choose
what they want to do.

What is each child doing?

The class rabbit has no name yet.

What would you like to call it?

Tell the story.

Match these big blocks with
the little blocks that have the same shape.

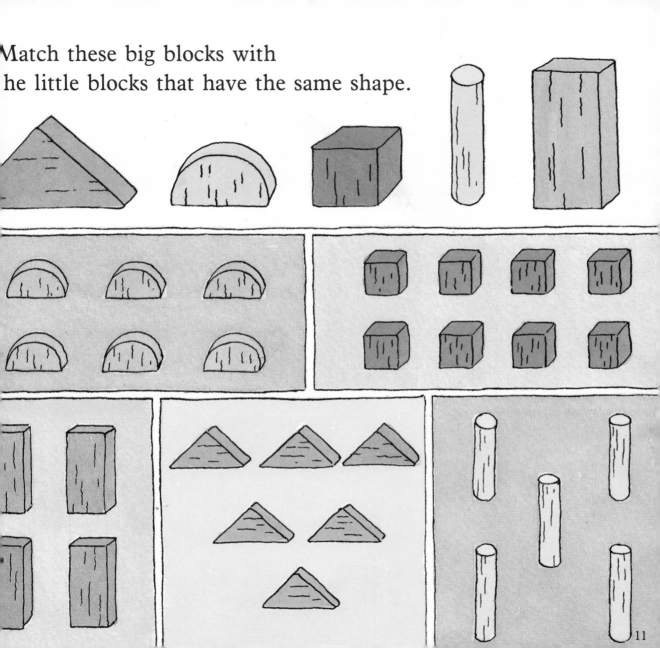

At meeting time everyone sits on an X.

Kate is telling about her new baby sister.

What do you think she is saying?

13

There are special activities in school.

music

science

movement

The playground is outside.

Can you find
all the tires?

15

Two children are painting.

Alden is making orange.

Bess is making green.

Which picture did Alden paint?

Which picture did Bess paint?

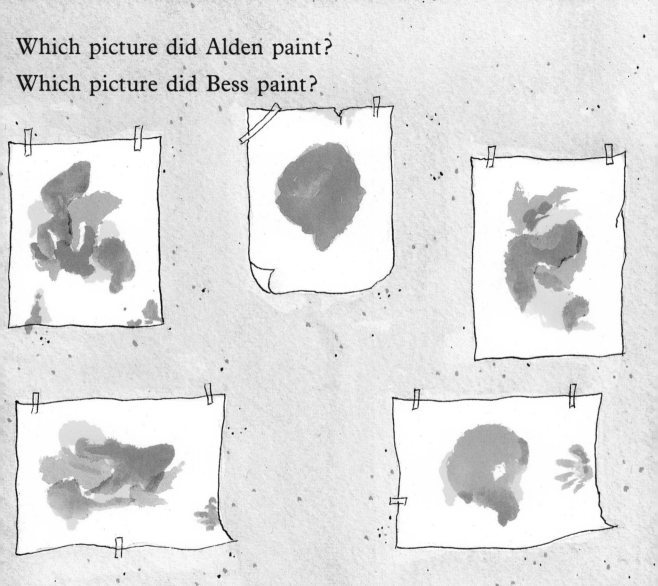

Can you say the names of all the colors?

BROOMS

Everyone uses the bathroom and washes up.

Snack time!

What are the children eating?

Do you know what these are for?

Every day one of the teachers reads a story.

hen school is over for the day.

he puppet sings, "Run along home."

"See you later, alligator!"

"So long till tomorrow!"

Say the alphabet.

A  B  C  D

J  K  L 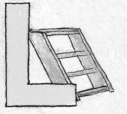 M

Can you find each thing again on another page?

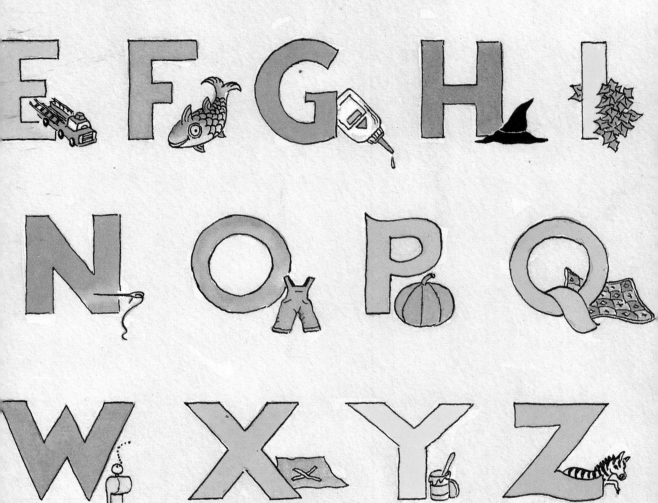

E F G H I

N O P Q

W X Y Z

27

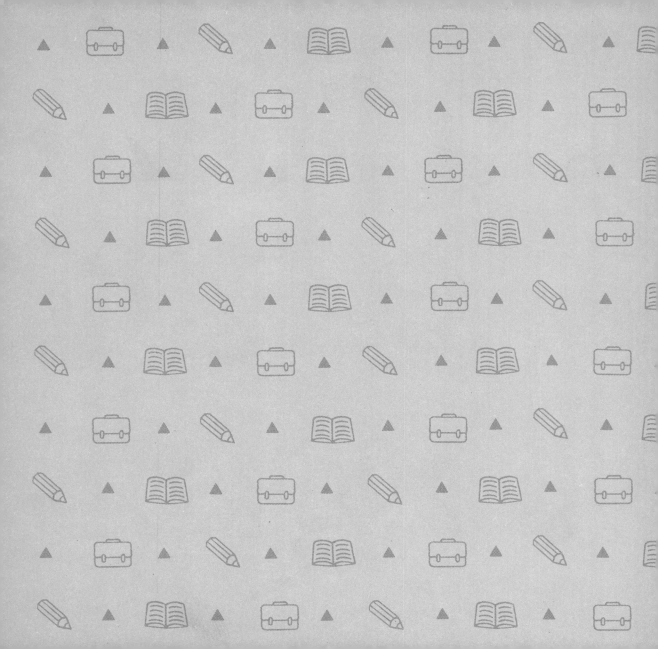

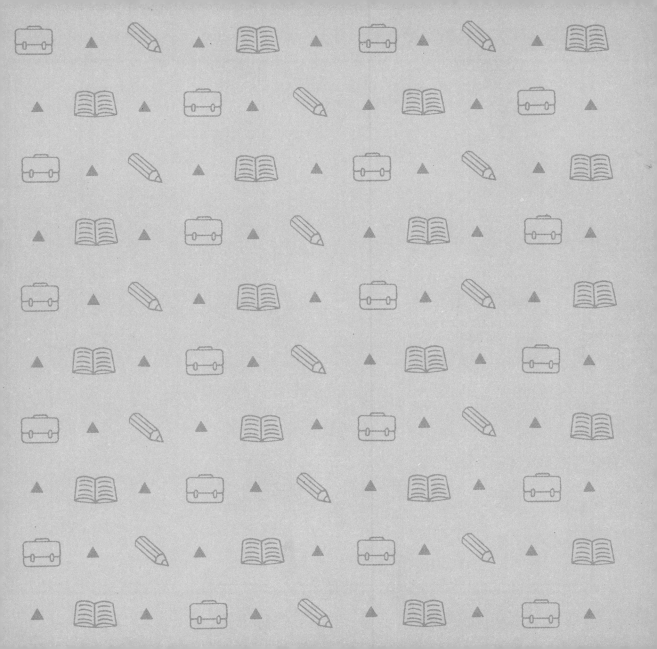